"This little book contains many good tips for co-creating a kinder working environment. Whether working from home or in a traditional workplace, we need to care and share and we need to build a sense of community. The new normal will likely see many of us working in a hybrid fashion — at home and in the office — and our challenges will be different again. That said, the need for community remains. In fact, it is all the more needed.

As Chairman of SKM, I worked with Dr Wan for a little over ten years. He is a practical visionary leader who can and does lead his team to achieve the goals he set out to achieve. He does it with kindness, and it works. Because he practises what he preaches, I treasure his thoughts. I commend his writings to you because I believe you will also find him relevant."

— Mr Koh Poh Tiong

Advisor & Board Director, Fraser and Neave, Limited

"There is no one who could not do with a dose of kindness to remind them they are human. Humanity in the workplace is embedded through leaders with a strong sense of personal and corporate purpose. With this sensibility, kindness is not peripheral but central to how leaders consider their impact on people and planet — and the legacy they leave behind."

— Ms Melissa Kwee

Chief Executive Officer, National Volunteer and Philanthropy Centre

"We believe that a brand's success is not based solely on its business achievements, but also by the positive role it plays in its community and environmental engagement. At Brands For Good, we recognise and honour SMEs across Asia for doing good.

Doing good embodies the principles of social responsibility in its business and operations, and that social responsibility assumes the practice of kindness by the people behind the organisations.

An organisation needs to care for its own staff before it can care for its stakeholders. Compassion, trust and respect are values that can positively impact employees, customers, and the communities an organisation operates and serves in.

Making Kindness Our Business encourages companies to take practical steps to create a kinder workplace, and in turn, a more gracious society where we can work, live and play.

A little kindness will go a long way in transforming our workplaces and communities for a better tomorrow."

er Wee

or Good

"It is sad we need this gem of a book. But we do. We value the wrong things like consumerism and materialism instead of our common humanity and decency. We forget to be considerate of others. This book reminds us why we should be consistently kind at work and at home."

— **Mr Victor Mills**
Chief Executive, Singapore International Chamber of Commerce

"Kindness underpins self-compassion, which is often overlooked yet key to fuel desire for self-improvement. Leaders who first show care and are kind toward self are more likely to set off virtuous spirals of humility, authenticity, and civility, which help till the ground for experimentation, and motivate their subordinates to want to do better, paving the way for eventual innovation."

— **Ms Jessica Shen**
Director, Human Resources & Organisation Development Division
Ministry of Culture, Community & Youth

"I have seen the positive impact of having a compassionate and inclusive work culture, not just for our colleagues, but also for our guests and stakeholders. Against the backdrop of pandemic burnout and the Great Resignation, Dr Wan's book elegantly captures the business imperative for being kind in today's world."

— **Ms Wee Wei Ling**
Executive Director, Sustainability Partnerships, Lifestyle & Asset
Pan Pacific Hotels Group

"For an organisation to succeed, there is a dire need to create a culture that engages the employees to have a positive experience by treating them well. This book offers practical tips and guidelines on real-life HR people issues in the new digitalisation and networking environment."

— **Dr Mohd Effendy Rajab**
Head (HR & Admin), Muhammadiyah Association

"This brilliant book by Dr William Wan has a powerful message for all of us: Kindness is good for mental health. The core values of synergy, kinship and positivity at the workplace bond colleagues and create a sense of belonging. Kindness to one another reduces stress, strengthens friendships, enhances feelings of confidence and optimism."

— **Professor Kua Ee Heok**
National University of Singapore

"My friend Dr Wan has written a practical volume about kindness at work. Each bite-sized chapter contains nuggets of wisdom and pragmatic suggestions that can be applied to organisations large and small. The "Discuss" pages at the end of each chapter provide a further opportunity to translate *Making Kindness Our Business* into tangible actions that are unique and relevant to each of us. His principles work, try them."

— **Ms Su-Yen Wong**
Chairperson, Singapore Institute of Directors

"In any workplace, being kind is and should be second nature. It will bring about harmony and happiness at the workplace and will lead to better service as a happy staff is more willing to go the extra mile for the company. Communication is critical and leaders must lead by example as kindness is reciprocal. The publication of *Making Kindness Our Business* is timely, especially during this pandemic where kindness and compassion are even more crucial to help your staff weather this challenging time and for them to know that you care."

— **Ms Margaret Heng**
Executive Director, Singapore Hotel Association

"Many points in this book resonated with me. Indeed, Best Workplaces™ in Singapore and around the world have a high-trust culture that would not be possible without kindness in the workplace. A great workplace is one in which employees trust the people they work for, have pride in their work, and experience camaraderie with their colleagues. Leaders are purpose-driven and adopt a people-first mindset so that employees' potential is maximized. This in turn contributes to a high-performing workplace. Treating one another with kindness and respect is fundamental to creating that great workplace. This makes it better for people, better for business and better for the world."

— **Ms Evelyn Kwek**
Managing Director, Great Place to Work® ASEAN & ANZ

"Dr William Wan has kindly gifted us a book of kindness at work. It is both informative yet practical, intellectually persuasive yet emotionally resonant, for reading pleasure and reflection pause. Dr Wan's global gift of kindness to readers worldwide makes a compelling business case for the cardinal importance of kindness. *Making Kindness Our Business* is an unstoppable kindness offensive for good that the world needs now."

— **Mr Gregory Vijendra**
Immediate Past President, Law Society of Singapore

"Keeping engagement high is important for workplaces. Simple acts of kindness have a positive impact on oneself and one's relationships at work. Kindness allows us to further embrace diversity and inclusion. This book contains simple and yet powerful tips for us to embrace kindness through acts like appreciation. Worth a read!"

— **Mr Johnathon Ng**
Vice President, Human Resources Asia Pacific
Brenntag Asia Pacific Pte Ltd

"As organisational consultants who promote values such as kindness, we encounter some who believe kindness belongs to charities, not businesses. This research-backed, comprehensive book is an antidote to such mindsets. Dr Wan shows that kindness is an essential part of being human and a wise foundation for successful leadership everywhere."

— **Ms Vadivu Govind**
Director, Human Unlimited

"The timeless message of kindness explored in this book is now more relevant than ever before. The Great Resignation has shown the cost to companies when employees are not supported by strong and empathetic leaders. Being kind doesn't just make good business sense; it is simply the right thing for leaders to do."

— **Mr Darrell Chan**
APAC General Counsel, Airbnb

"The heartbeat of a company comes from a workplace culture that treats employees with kindness and fairness. In today's modern economy, work-life harmony is critical to employee welfare. When a company creates a flexible family-friendly workplace, it benefits both employers and staff, such as working mums who constantly juggle responsibilities at work and at home. *Making Kindness Our Business* encourages employers and employees to rethink the 'heart' of a company. The goal? To create a more progressive workplace for working caregivers, parents-to-be, mothers of young children and those returning to full-time work. In doing so, we can help every employee realise their full potential."

— **Ms Yeo Wan Ling**
Director, U SME and U Women & Family
National Trades Union Congress (NTUC)

MAKING KINDNESS OUR BUSINESS

How Kindness at Work Can Lead to
Happier, More Engaged Workers

William Wan

Marshall Cavendish
Business

Published in 2022 by Marshall Cavendish Business
An imprint of Marshall Cavendish International

A member of the
Times Publishing Group

Other Marshall Cavendish Offices:
Marshall Cavendish Corporation, 800 Westchester Ave, Suite N-641, Rye Brook, NY 10573, USA • Marshall Cavendish International (Thailand) Co Ltd, 253 Asoke, 16th Floor, Sukhumvit 21 Road, Klongtoey Nua, Wattana, Bangkok 10110, Thailand • Marshall Cavendish (Malaysia) Sdn Bhd, Times Subang, Lot 46, Subang Hi-Tech Industrial Park, Batu Tiga, 40000 Shah Alam, Selangor Darul Ehsan, Malaysia

Marshall Cavendish is a registered trademark of Times Publishing Limited

NATIONAL LIBRARY BOARD, SINGAPORE CATALOGUING IN PUBLICATION DATA
Name(s): Wan, William.
Title: Making kindness our business : how kindness at work can lead to happier, more engaged workers / William Wan.
Description: Singapore : Marshall Cavendish Business, 2022.
Identifier(s): ISBN 978-981-4974-24-0 (paperback)
Subject(s): LCSH: Kindness. | Employees--Psychology. | Employee motivation. | Organizational behavior.
Classification: DDC 658.314--dc23

Printed in Singapore

Contents

III. Leadership

IV. Teamwork

V. Corporate Social Responsibility

VI. The Digital Workplace

VII. The Post-pandemic Workplace

Minister's Message

We spend so much of our lives at work, so how can we improve our well-being and enjoy the interactions that we have with others?

This publication brings us a step closer to that goal – it emphasises that a workplace culture based on an ethos of kindness is essential. An organisation's success depends on mutual trust and understanding between employees and employers. Kindness helps lay the foundation for this trust, and this book shares different ways in which employers can show kindness to their employees, and employees to each other.

How we reach out to one another and show solidarity with others will define who we are as a society. Translating this into action in the work environment means we need to examine the values and practices that drive our businesses, so that we can align and achieve both business value creation and broad-based prosperity in the long term.

This means creating a culture of kindness with supporting policies that protect workers and reinforcing networks of care and support within our organisations, in order to respond to the stresses and precarity arising from complex challenges like the pandemic.

Many businesses are already finding out, at a large cost to themselves, that kindness is not a luxury, but a necessity. In turn, those who have found strength in kindness have grown stronger.

Dr William Wan, in this collection of essays, shows us how a culture of kindness in our own micro-communities might pave the way for a more cohesive and confident nation overall, and "be the measure of success that really matters".

Mr Edwin Tong
Minister for Culture, Community and Youth
& Second Minister for Law
Adviser, Singapore Kindness Movement

Chairperson's Message

Covid-19 has changed the landscape of workplaces in Singapore and all over the world.

Yet despite Zoom meetings and work-from-home procedures, kindness remains key to a healthy, engaged and more productive workplace.

At the Singapore Kindness Movement, we aim to inspire graciousness through spontaneous acts of kindness to make life more pleasant for everyone. Our goals are simple: To encourage all Singaporeans to be kind and considerate, to create public awareness of acts of kindness, and to influence and raise the standards of social behaviour and responsibility.

Since 2013, SKM has been promoting the Kindness@Work programme – an initiative to generate happier and more gracious workplace environments in Singapore.

The theme for our "Be Greater" campaign redefines kindness as the measure of success, not the usual comparisons of wealth, status and power.

It also challenges Singaporeans to go beyond random acts of kindness to better ourselves through a consideration of our individual and collective values.

We can all exemplify this through purposeful acts of kindness within our own spheres of influence in ordinary everyday settings – such as our workplaces.

We invite corporate leaders to implement Kindness@Work – through webinars and organisational resources – for better mental and emotional wellness, similar to how healthy lifestyle programmes have become de rigueur in human resource management.

We have made good progress in the past 23 years, but we still have a long way to go for Singapore to be a gracious society, and the change has to start with each one of us as individuals.

To our corporate partners, thank you for joining us on this journey for kindness. Because of your support and participation, we are closer to our goal to make Singapore a better place for everyone to live, work and play in.

True greatness is not about what we achieve, but the kind of nation and people we strive to be – one that we can take pride in.

We look forward to working together with all of you to make Kindness@Work happen in your respective organisations. I wish you all the best in your kind endeavours.

Ms Junie Foo
Chairperson, Singapore Kindness Movement

Foreword

Back in 2015, as an INSPIRIT member, I received an invitation to be a council member for a non-profit. I swear I gave a delighted squeal when I heard that it was for the Singapore Kindness Movement and I guess the person on the line figured that I was interested.

Singa and I go way back. When I was in primary school, I won a few competitions where the prizes were Singa collectibles under the National Courtesy Campaign. No prizes for guessing my age, by the way!

I have always wanted to be part of a movement whose key motivation is to spread kindness. In a world that has so much negativity in the media, how do you not want to be a part of something so wonderfully positive?

Though my answer was an immediate resounding YES, I still had to meet the Dr Wan-derful to ensure that we had a connection and that I would be a good fit for the council.

Well, here I am, penning the foreword for this book on kindness at work, not just as an SKM council member, but as its Secretary and to an extent, collaborator, given that the articles in this book first appeared in the magazine that I am Editor of, *Today's Manager*.

The importance of understanding why we need to be kind

not only to our peers, but to our staff too, has never been more critical. We need to understand that everyone who works does it as they have mouths to feed.

I have seen some companies where kindness is so embedded within their DNA it must be an absolute joy to work there.

If companies understand the importance of creating an environment where the employees feel like they are going to their second home instead of just going to earn a living, these employees will develop a sense of passion and drive that will produce results naturally.

Therein lies the importance of the Kindness@Work programme. It was so heartening to see many from top management attend these talks run by the SKM.

I was fortunate to have been the guest of honour at one of these talks, even giving a welcome speech to everyone who attended.

I hope to see kindness at work continue, even becoming part of the modus operandi, instead of merely chasing dollars and cents. If you care about your people, if you help them see the value of caring for their peers and their staff, the results you will reap will be the success that you are gunning for.

Read this book with an open mind and open heart, as the wise words apply to any level – not just at top or senior management levels. Anyone can apply kindness at work.

And if you need help, SKM is but an email, phone call, or social media message away. We would be more than pleased to visit you at your office or hold an online Zoom session. As Zoom-bified as your colleagues might feel, trust me, listening to Dr Wan will be worth their while.

I wish you the very best and I truly hope you make the most of this book. Show the world that you can be greater by being kinder.

Dr Sadie-Jane Nunis
Secretary, Singapore Kindness Movement Council
Editor, *Today's Manager*

Introduction

This year marks my eighth year working at the Singapore Kindness Movement.

At the beginning of my SKM journey, I often felt weird telling people this is what I do because almost always they would respond, "So you must be very kind then!"

I would usually laugh it off.

The truth is, working at a charity that celebrates generosity and kindness doesn't automatically make a person kind. Our jobs are very similar to that of many of you who work in an office environment – although we do distribute a massive number of yellow gerbera daisies once a year on Kindness Day SG!

But I have learnt that kindness does make a difference in the workplace, and I have seen its benefits.

I am thankful to be in a supportive team where I am able to grow both professionally and personally. It also helps that my bosses appreciate and recognise my work.

When there is a culture of kindness, team members are more engaged and productive, and they look forward to going to work (even if it's at home!).

I will admit, it has not been an easy task approaching companies to adopt our programmes. In today's fast-paced, highly competitive world, kindness can be seen as a nicety that is "good to have" but not necessary, perhaps even unimportant compared to increasing the bottom line.

However, I am encouraged that through running the Kindness@Work programme with our corporate partners, we are helping to change perceptions of how kindness can create positive change.

This book will share practical ways on how you can do so, both personally and professionally.

Recently, I received an unexpected sweet treat from a colleague I had not physically seen in months because of Covid-19 restrictions. We used to go for lunch together back in the office and it was lovely catching up with her and finding out how she has been coping with WFH.

It reminded me that as humans, we all have a need to connect and build relationships with one another. And this is true especially at the workplace, where we spend more waking hours than at home.

We are often too shy to take the first step. But once that barrier is brought down, there is so much kindness to give and receive. We just need to be brave enough to reach out.

I hope this book will inspire you to take your first step to be greater – in your workplace and in your personal life.

Ms Serene Leong
Assistant Editor, *The Pride*
Singapore Kindness Movement

To find out more about the Kindness@Work programme for your organisation, email kindness@kindness.sg

Kindness Is Good for Business

*Kindness and performance are not mutually exclusive.
Practising kindness and graciousness at work can lead to
better performance and profitability.*

In today's fast-paced and highly competitive business landscape, kindness appears to be irrelevant. It can almost be seen as a hindrance that slows us down and dulls our competitive edge. That is what some may think. But I would like to suggest that kindness is good for business and is more relevant than we think.

MAKING KINDNESS OUR BUSINESS

Many behavioural studies have shown that practising acts of kindness has a positive effect on a person's happiness, satisfaction in relationships, and even one's physical and mental health.

Here's the science. When we are kind to others, our brains "reward" us by releasing a mixture of chemicals, including dopamine, oxytocin, and serotonin, which makes us feel good.[1] In fact, it has been found that doing a kind act not only bestows a sense of satisfaction on the receiver, but also on the one who performed the act, and all those who witnessed it.

But what does that have to do with achieving business objectives? What is the benefit to us as employers and employees who practise kindness and graciousness in the workplace? Is it simply something that is "good to have" but not essential, or deemed unimportant, compared to the need to scale up our performance and increase the bottom-line?

The truth is, kindness and performance are not mutually exclusive. In fact, practising kindness and graciousness at work can lead to better performance and profitability. Researchers have found that happy workers who enjoy their work and have fun working together perform their jobs better.

Professor Teresa Amabile and Steve Kramer of Harvard Business School found that "People are more productive, creative, committed, and collegial when they have positive emotions… and when they are motivated by intrinsic interest in the work itself."[2]

According to The Huffington Post, "66 per cent surveyed say that positive relationships increased their productivity and 55 per cent say that positive relationships mitigate on-the-job stress levels".[3]

When kindness and graciousness are deeply rooted in the corporate culture, the business will profit from higher levels of employee engagement, greater synergy and loyalty, and more fulfilling working relationships. This translates into a more motivated workforce and lower staff turnover, so employers can better retain talent. Furthermore, engaged and invested employees will be more proactive in innovating and creating solutions for the organisation, whether these are for external marketing or internal processes.

The net result is higher profitability in more ways than one. In sum, kindness is good for business.

DISCUSS

What are three ways a kinder workplace can benefit your business?

What immediate steps can you take to create a kinder workplace in your organisation?

Make a commitment to do something kind for someone at work.

Think Positively, Act Kindly

*Managing with kindness releases and regenerates the
positivity that we need to succeed.*

I was honoured to be interviewed for two books about leadership.[4] Though the interviewees come from diverse backgrounds, we all share a positive outlook on life and work: none of us approaches our professional goals with anything less than a "can do" attitude.

Kindness is my passion. It energises me because it is a positive energy. I have been positive for as far as I can remember and refuse to let negative people or circumstances in life dampen my spirit for too long.

There are at least three big road bumps that I had to overcome to get me to where I am today. In the early 70s, I started a law firm with two other partners. One of them split from us within the first year, insisting on his right to take over our newly renovated offices and keep the best of our staff. We had a choice: either resist and spend our energy fighting back, or give him our blessings and walk away. We chose the latter and decided not to waste good energy fighting him. We let go and restarted successfully.

Then in the early 90s, one of my daughters, a bright student, decided to drop out of school in the pursuit of a hedonistic lifestyle in a far-off country. We let her go but loved her unconditionally and kept our door wide open. She came back seven years later, returned to school as a single mother, and earned her PhD.

The final road bump was getting fired from a senior leadership position at age 51. Refusing to roll over and expire, I returned to law practice after 25 years and made a success of it. The organisation that fired me has since publicly apologised.

I overcame problems big and small with a good measure of kindness wrapped with a good spread of forgiveness. A kindness mindset of letting passing things pass liberates me from the past so that I can fully live life in the present and positively look forward to the future.

Research by Barbara L. Fredrickson,[5] a psychology professor from the University of Michigan, found that those who think positive thoughts have a greater capacity to take on board new information and build their skill sets. It changes a person's perspective and ability to "connect the dots", which in turn enables them to tackle any problems and obstacles that may arise.

I was able to reinvent myself many times over because I practised the positivity of kindness. Kindness gives me positive dispositional affect so that I have more energy and enthusiasm to be more productive. It gives me the resilience I need to recover from negative experiences. As Professor Fredrickson writes, "positive emotions help speed recovery from negative emotions", even if the positive thinking is self-generated.

A recent study has confirmed that positive thinking improves decision-making. In the seminal book, *Understanding the Entrepreneurial Mind*,[6] the researchers emphasised the point that "negative thinking from entrepreneurs in a negative mood could lead to decisions which are more likely to be poor for their venture". Needless to say, the antidote is positive thinking.

That is why managing with kindness releases and regenerates the positivity that we need to succeed.

DISCUSS

What is one challenge you are currently facing in your personal or professional life?

How can you turn this challenge into an opportunity for success?

What is one positive thought you hope to put into practice?

3

Happiness at Work Is Not a Lost Cause

When you feel unmotivated or overwhelmed by a task at work, challenge yourself to do something kind for someone else, and see the difference it makes.

In today's fast-paced society, many people show up at work each day without feeling emotionally invested in what they do. The stress of the daily grind can create a cycle of low motivation, dwindling productivity, and escalating unhappiness.

This is not surprising as Singaporeans work some of the longest hours among workers in the world's most developed countries, according to a study by Dutch researchers. Singapore's average of 2,287 hours per year is much higher than Japan's 1,706 or the United States' 1,703. We are only behind Hong Kong's 2,344.

According to a 2012 survey conducted by JobsCentral, two out of three Singaporean workers indicated that their workload had increased in the past six months and that stress levels had risen in the same period. Forty per cent of Singapore workers polled named office politics as a major stressor; 35 per cent cited workload, and 35 per cent felt that they lacked support.[7]

While there will always be pressure to perform and deadlines to meet, happiness at the workplace is not a lost cause if kindness is its starting point.

Research has shown a clear link between kindness and happiness. A 2006 study published in the *Journal of Happiness Studies* confirmed that doing a kind act bestows a sense of satisfaction not only on the receiver, but also on the one who performs the act and those who witness it. Kindness releases a mixture of chemicals (including dopamine and serotonin) in our brain, making us feel good.[8]

Researchers studying employee motivation and well-being have also found that happiness at work is not so much a function of salary, benefits, or job titles, but rather the relationships fostered at the workplace.[9]

Since most of us spend more than half of our waking hours in the office, the quality of interaction with our colleagues and superiors greatly influences our perception of the workplace environment.

A Gallup report on "The State of The American Workplace"[10] has found that strong social connections at the office can boost productivity – making employees more passionate about their work and less likely to quit their jobs.

How can we promote a supportive work environment where management and staff enjoy a greater give-and-take relationship that is mutually beneficial, set each other up for success, and help one another get through the day-to-day challenges of work?

First of all, managers can pave the way by treating employees with respect, empathy, and compassion, so that employees feel valued and appreciated. This creates a fair, collaborative, and open culture where employees are more empowered to be ambitious and creative.

Likewise, employees should also return the same kindness and appreciation to their managers by exercising integrity and pride to produce excellent work. In this way, a virtuous cycle of kindness can boost morale and heighten the motivation to excel.

In the Singapore Kindness Movement, even though our team is split to cover several sectors, we encourage everyone to support one another's projects and events – whether by guiding, sharing past experiences, or simply being on-site to lend a helping hand.

Simple acts of kindness like greeting one another, smiling more often, and saying "Thanks" to one another can go a long way in creating a happier work environment. Such acts are even known to reduce work stress.

If practised on a daily basis, such acts can promote a culture where people are quick to recognise and return the kind and thoughtful gestures of others.

In fact, there are studies that show a "positive feedback loop" between kindness and happiness. When we are kind, we become happier, and the happier we feel, the more likely we are to do another kind act.[11] And people who engage in kind acts become happier over time.[12]

Kindness is a simple concept to practise. Perhaps one might think that kindness is too simple a solution to the complex challenges we face at the workplace today. Yet it could be the elusive key to achieving happiness at work.

The next time you find your motivation dwindling or feel overwhelmed by a task at work, challenge yourself to do something kind for someone else, and see what a difference it makes!

DISCUSS

On a scale of 1 to 10, how happy are you at work? Why do you think so?

Think of the last time you felt happy at work. What encouraged this positive feeling?

How can you create "a fair, collaborative, and open culture where employees are more empowered to be ambitious and creative"?

4

Are You Kind to Yourself?

*Embodying kindness impacts others around us, but we
should not forget to be kind to ourselves too.*

Many organisations participate in corporate social responsibility (CSR) through volunteer programmes and donation
schemes. These efforts encourage us to be kind to others. Yet, in
our attempts to do good, we have often forgotten to be kind to
ourselves.

Workplace stress is on the increase. A 2016 study by Rof-
frey Park found that not only did Singapore workers spend more
hours at work relative to their Hong Kong and China peers, but

more than half (52 per cent of Singapore workers surveyed) said their stress level had gone up over the past six months.[13] There is a co-relation between our work habits and stress.

We are certainly not kind to ourselves if we stress ourselves out. Before we can be kind to others, we should first be kind to ourselves. Being kind is a way of making our own lives, and the lives of others, meaningful. It allows us to communicate better with others, be more self-compassionate, and also be a positive force in other people's lives.

There are many health benefits when we are kind to ourselves. Research has found that people who practise self-love and compassion not only experience less stress, but have a lower heart rate, lower blood pressure, and a stronger immune system.[14]

Happy, balanced, and successful people practise self-love and compassion. Here are three ways to practise kindness to ourselves in the context of the workplace.

1. Bring Your Whole, Authentic Self to Work

Many of us are too concerned with what our colleagues and bosses think and expect of us. To impress others, we put on a façade that is not our true self. By doing that, we subject ourselves to the stress of living a double life. This may hinder us from truly being happy and successful at work.

Authentic people are genuine and consistently true to themselves. They know what they value and they are purpose-driven. They are not embarrassed to show their true self to others, and others feel safe and comfortable in their presence.

We can take small steps to start being more authentic. Find a time where you and your colleagues can share about things outside of work – your values, culture, hobbies, aspirations and family – without being judgemental.

2. Build Resilience to Better Handle Life and Work Challenges

What makes some people persevere through trying circumstances while others begin flailing at the first sign of crisis? Research shows that resilient people think differently. They have a set of skills (both learned and innate) that allows them to persevere, manage stress, and triumph in the face of challenges.[15]

Resilient people have strong reserves of inner and outer strength. They are consistently conscious of seeking new ways to build strong personal foundations so they may weather the storms of life and work. They do this through increasing their awareness of how to care for themselves physically, emotionally, and spiritually.

In the pursuit of excellence and success, we are vulnerable to stress and burnout. Keeping our mind and body healthy is one way to handle that vulnerability.

Taking time for self-care includes intentionally carving out time for yourself every day and doing something that brings you joy. Facing each day with a heart of gratitude helps us to be thankful for what we have, and motivates us to become happier and stronger individuals.

3. Maintain a Positive Attitude

People with positive attitudes are optimistic no matter what the circumstances are, and they exude enthusiasm and confidence in their actions and words. They approach life as a learning journey, believing they are in control of their lives. They choose how they should respond to their surroundings, looking for the best in any situation.

Studies have shown that people with positive attitudes also tend to be more productive at work.[16] This is because they see the opportunity with every challenge. They have greater resilience and have the ability to inspire and motivate themselves and others.

On the other hand, a negative person cultivates thoughts that drain them of energy and keep them from being in the present moment. They focus on the flaws in situations, and are generally moody, grumpy, or cynical.

We choose the attitude with which we view our work. And this determines how much we enjoy our jobs and the people we interact with at work.

It is never too late to start being kind to ourselves. When we embody kindness from within, we will start to see that it naturally impacts those around us, and we will find it easier to be kind to others.

DISCUSS

Do you find it difficult to be kind to yourself? Why or why not?

What is one thing you can do to be kinder to yourself today?

How can you better manage stress at work so as to prevent burnout?

5

Lead With Kindness, You Will Get Better Results

Kind leaders are able to focus on both the bottom-line and the needs of their people, and finish first with the right approach and strategy.

Kindness does not spontaneously come to mind when we think of business or leadership. One might even believe that being kind may hamper your progress at work or cause others to take advantage of you. However, I would submit that strong leadership and kindness are not mutually exclusive.

In *Leading with Kindness*, the authors William Baker and Michael O'Malley state at the outset: "In order for companies to improve, the people of the organisations have to become smarter and more resourceful and work together more effectively over time. For this to work, people actually have to care about their work, the company, and one another. This requires the expert orchestration of a kind leader."[17]

The most successful leaders treat their team members with kindness. They realise that kindness is motivating, earns the trust and respect of their people, and leads to better results.

But first, you might ask, what is a kind leader?

A kind leader is not a permissive person or pushover.[18] Being a kind leader does not mean that you don't fire people. It doesn't mean that you don't make tough decisions that will impact the bottom-line. It simply means that you are focused as much on the delivery of your message as you are on the message itself.

Kindness is also not likeability. When you focus on being liked, you will instinctively try to please the people you are leading. And you will end up bending over backwards to make everyone happy. You will never have the courage to do what needs to be done.[19]

John Keyser, founder of Common Sense Leadership, defines a kind leader as "being a person of character and demonstrating an unwavering commitment to the learning, growth, and success of others".[20]

Kind leaders relate to their people with genuine care, and are dedicated to helping them succeed. We rise by lifting others. This manner of leadership invigorates the culture of our organisation and inspires our people to also care about one another, valuing team accomplishments over personal achievements.

How then does kindness contribute to strong and effective leadership?

Firstly, kindness engages and motivates employees. Researchers from the New York University Stern School of Business[21] found that when leaders are self-sacrificing, their employees experience being moved and inspired. As a consequence, the employees feel more loyal and committed and are more likely to go out of their way to be helpful and friendly to other employees.

Secondly, kindness earns the trust and respect of people. Researchers from Harvard Business School[22] have shown that leaders who project kindness and warmth (even before establishing their competence) are more effective than those who lead with their toughness and skill. One reason is trust.

For a team of colleagues, trust can increase productivity by altering how we react to motivation to achieve results. Trust also plays a surprising role in communication – we are more likely to hold back our own feelings about an issue when we don't trust the person we are sharing information with.

To be a highly effective leader, we want to strive to earn and maintain the respect and trust of our team members. When we have their trust and respect, they will believe in you and the organisation's cause, and do their best for the team.

There is no doubt that kindness is good for business. Kind leaders are able to focus on both the bottom-line and on the needs of their people. And contrary to popular belief, with the right approach and strategy, kind leaders actually finish first.

DISCUSS

What makes a kind leader and what doesn't make a kind leader?

What is one thing you can practise as a leader to earn and maintain the respect and trust of your team members?

How can you be a role model for your team members?

6

Why "Be Greater" Is Important for Our Society

When we look out for opportunities around us, kindness can become second nature.

WHILE YOU SET YOUR SIGHTS ON SUCCESS, DON'T LOSE SIGHT OF THE THINGS THAT MAKE US HUMAN. BE GREATER.

Wealth, success, and power have been the key defining factors of greatness in Singapore society.

Singapore is known for its stable economy, world-class infra-structure, excellent housing, education, and healthcare systems – the envy of many countries. We also have one of the highest gross domestic product (GDP) per capita and income in the world.

Yet, Singaporeans do not seem to be happy. Singapore has the highest depression rate in Asia, according to a 2015 study by the World Health Organization.

In our pursuit of prosperity and progress, have we forgotten how to be happy and how to care for each other as a nation?

True Greatness Is More than Wealth, Success, and Power

It is important for Singapore as a nation to shift its narrative when it comes to our definition and pursuit of greatness.

True greatness is about character and a better version of ourselves beyond success, wealth, and power.

More than that, greatness is about the kindness that is in us. And we can all exemplify this through purposeful acts of kindness within our own circles, in very ordinary settings such as our workplaces, neighbourhoods, and homes.

"Be Greater" Is a Personal Choice

Everyday situations present opportunities for us to be kind, whether it is giving way to another driver on the road, lending a helping hand to someone in need, or encouraging a friend with kind words.

Motorcyclist Mr Angelo was on the road one night when he encountered an elderly, wheelchair-bound man trying with difficulty to cross the road. Without any hesitation, Mr Angelo got off his bike and helped to push the man across the road.

"It only takes a few seconds to be kind to others, and it can change someone's day," said Mr Angelo. "It can even create a ripple effect where others are inspired to be kind to those around them too."

Being greater is easily achievable by all. When we look out for opportunities around us, and choose kindness, giving and receiving kindness can become second nature. We become less hindered by doubt or self-consciousness. Kindness becomes part of a national identity that Singaporeans can take pride in.

The findings from Singapore Kindness Movement's latest Graciousness Survey show that more youths aspire to make an impact in creating a greater community. Some have responded to the call to be greater in their own ways.

Undergraduate Adrian Foo started a project collecting five-cent coins from friends, family, and even strangers, to raise funds and awareness for needy cardboard collectors. More than 14,000 coins, worth S$709, were collected and donated.

"It is really heartening to see what we can do for the community when we all come together to contribute," wrote Mr Foo in a Facebook post. "No amount of contribution is too small."

There are more of such stories on *The Pride*, which showcase real-life Singaporeans defying the bystander effect and stepping up to help when the situation calls for it.

These stories are slowly helping to change the narrative that one must have more material possessions and achievements to be successful and happy.

We Cannot Choose to be Happy, but We Can Choose to be Kind

If we centre our lives around material possessions for our self-enjoyment, we will be unhappy because scientific studies show that beyond a certain amount that we need, money does not add on to our happiness.

At the end of the day, life is about relationships, not about money. Money is only an extension of our ability to share and care.

In July 2019, in partnership with *The Straits Times*, SKM organised a panel discussion which debated the question: "Why should the privileged give back to society? And how?"

The aim was to start a national conversation for Singaporeans to reflect on what it means to be privileged, and how we can help others in different ways.

With self-awareness, empathy, and contentment with what we have, we can be more conscious, deliberate, and specific in our giving, resulting in an ongoing process of mutual care and everyone giving to each other as we are able.

A Positive Feedback Loop Between Kindness and Happiness

Paradoxically, in being other-centred, we benefit ourselves in the process. When we are kind, we become happier, and the happier we feel, the more likely we are to do another kind act. And people who engage in kind acts become happier over time.

When we place more emphasis on kindness, graciousness, and other-centredness, happiness naturally comes as a by-product.

If each of us can choose to be greater in our individual lives, in our own capacity and form, imagine what the collective impact could be for our society!

True greatness is not about what we achieve, but about the kind of people we strive to be. Together, we can Be Greater.

DISCUSS

Are Singaporeans happy? Why or why not?

How can we change the narrative that one must have more in terms of possessions and achievements to be successful and happy?

Should the privileged give back to society? How can we do so?

7

What Do Kindness and Camaraderie Have in Common?

Together, kindness and camaraderie help to shape the fabric of a work culture that inspires productivity.

Camaraderie between employees undisputedly helps to create a happier and more positive workplace. Many organisations are generating camaraderie by spending time and resources organising staff lunches, birthday celebrations, and team-building sessions.

Such activities create higher employee engagement and loyalty.

Researchers have found that happiness at work is not so much a function of salary, benefits, or job titles. A key contributor to workplace happiness is the relationships that are fostered there.[23]

Since many of us spend more than half of our waking hours at work, interactions with our colleagues and superiors inevitably determine our sense of well-being.

A Gallup report on "The State of The American Workplace"[24] states that strong social connections at the office can boost productivity, and could make employees more passionate about their work and less likely to quit their jobs.

Treating co-workers with kindness helps to build camaraderie and trust, both of which are key components of successful and synergistic teamwork.

When we work with teammates who have each other's back and set one another up for success, we leverage on our collective talents and perspectives to work together towards a common vision. We will also generate more energy and enthusiasm for the work we do.[25]

At the Singapore Kindness Movement, we practise three internal core values: Synergy, Kinship, and (positive) Mindset. We are convinced that Together Each Achieves More (TEAM). Though we each have our own sector and primary focus, we give permission to call on one another to help in our respective sectors when there is a need. We make it a habit to ask each other: "How can I set you up for success?"

We also believe in building a bond where we learn to care for and share with one another. We believe that when we enjoy working together and still have fun achieving our collective passion, we achieve a sense of well-being and become more productive. We look forward to work because we enjoy both the work and the people we work with.

Camaraderie is more than just having fun; it is about creating a shared sense of purpose. Studies have confirmed that soldiers form strong bonds during missions in part because they believe in the purpose of the mission, rely on each other, and share the good and the bad as a team.[26]

Camaraderie presupposes goodwill towards one another. Treating each other with respect, empathy, and compassion, and valuing and appreciating one another are necessary pieces in the cultural fabric of kindness. Such reciprocal conduct creates a positive feedback loop that boosts morale and heightens the motivation to excel.

Though we may be colleagues by chance, we can be friends by choice. Friendship gives us a sense of belonging and helps us pull through the daily challenges of work and life.

Kindness and camaraderie go together like the two blades on a pair of scissors. Together, they are a simple tool to shape the fabric of a work culture that inspires productivity.

DISCUSS

What contributes to your workplace happiness?

How can you be a friend at work?

How can you encourage camaraderie among team members while working from home?

8

Building a Culture of Appreciation and Gratitude: Part 1

When were you last recognised for a job well done?
Do you commend others for doing a good job?

No matter who we are in the totem pole of seniority in our organisation, we feel good when we get complimented. It could be as simple as a smile, a pat on the shoulder, a "thank you", or an elaborate commendation ceremony. Appreciation is always appreciated!

Appreciation not only makes the workplace happier and

kinder, it makes business sense too. Appreciated employees are more likely to be positive, engaged, high-performing, and have better retention rates.

According to Gallup, recognition motivates 82 per cent of employees to improve their job performance. A top factor for raising overall employee engagement is regular praise from managers.[27]

In addition, showing gratitude towards co-workers creates more social and prosocial interaction. People who participated in gratitude exercises were found to be more prosocial than others."[28] The Positive Psychology Programme defines prosocial as "promoting other's well-being usually through altruistic acts".

A few months ago, SKM embarked on a programme aimed at cultivating "Love, Growth, and Gratitude" in the workplace. One of the activities involved a daily gratitude sharing within small groups across different departments for one week.

Doing this simple exercise daily to reflect and write down the things I am grateful for helped me to be aware of the many blessings I am given each day. It encouraged the team to have a positive mindset as we face the challenges both in and outside of work.

Through this gratitude sharing, we were able to share in each other's joys and struggles. Often, we don't get to know our colleagues outside of work, especially those whom we may not interact with on a daily basis. At the end of the day, everyone is fighting their own battles. A simple conversation asking a teammate "How are you?" to show care and concern can help bring a human touch to today's fast-paced, technology-centric, impersonal workplace environment.

Studies have shown that appreciation and gratitude generate significant positive effects on employees' well-being and health.

Showing gratitude can increase a person's wellness, promote better sleep habits, increase metabolism, and reduce stress. Scientifically, the hypothalamus – the part of the brain that controls basic bodily functions such as eating and sleeping – and dopamine, the "reward neurotransmitter", are heavily affected by feelings of gratitude.[29] A recent Gallup poll highlighted "a gap between what a company thinks it is doing to appreciate great work, and what its employees see happening on a day-to-day basis. Only seven per cent of employees say their company is excellent at appreciating great work, while 56 per cent of management say their company is above average at appreciation, and nearly 80 per cent mention lack of appreciation as a key reason for leaving their jobs. Employees want some form of recognition every seven days, but research shows that just over 50 per cent of leaders recognise their employees once a quarter or less".[30]

The good news is that there is a shift in the perceived sense of community. Dr Vanessa Buote writes in a Plasticity Labs white paper titled "Gratitude at Work: Its Impact on Job Satisfaction and Sense of Community" that "with more and more companies focusing on collaboration and team effort, building a sense of community among co-workers is crucial – and one way to do so is through gratitude".[31] Besides, expressing gratitude not only makes the receiver feel good, but also the "thanker": 88 per cent of employees reported that expressing gratitude to colleagues makes them feel happy and fulfilled, and our research reveals that both giving and receiving support is linked to job satisfaction, engagement, and happiness".[32] There is absolutely no question that an attitude of gratitude is not only good for our personal health and well-being, it is also good for the health and well-being of the corporation.

DISCUSS

When were you last appreciated or recognised for a job well done? How did you feel?

How can you show appreciation to your colleagues and bosses?

What is one thing you can do to cultivate an attitude of gratitude?

9

Building a Culture of Appreciation and Gratitude: Part 2

Being grateful has benefits to personal and corporate health and well-being.

Having an attitude of gratitude is undoubtedly not only good for our personal health and well-being, but also for the health and well-being of a corporation. How can we then create a culture of appreciation and gratitude in our workplaces? Here are some ways to do it.

First of all, as with every organisational change, it starts from the top. Managers and leaders can set the tone for employees by practising acts of appreciation such as giving immediate feedback for a job well done, writing a thank-you card, or even dropping a simple email to thank them specifically for what it is you appreciate. Let them know how it helped you and the company.

Appreciation does not have to be a grand gesture or a huge promotion. A little recognition from leaders goes a long way toward employee satisfaction and motivation. Something as simple as making time to stop by an employee's desk to speak to them face-to-face can help close the communication gap and empower employees to perform better in their roles. It allows them to feel that their hard work and sacrifices are understood and valued.

In fact, according to a survey by Kelton Research, nearly 50 per cent of working Americans say they would rather be appreciated than have an opportunity to advance in their careers.[33] The study also found, with escalating workplace demands, employees aren't feeling valued by superiors.[34] It is indeed dismaying that a Gallup research shows 70 per cent of working Americans receive no praise or recognition on the job.[35]

Another way to build a culture of appreciation in the workplace is to create physical spaces in the office where co-workers can express their appreciation and thanks for one another, and even to their bosses. Such spaces are called "Kindness Corners" or "Thank You Corners".

By exercising kindness and recognising others' acts of kindness, a growing cycle of kindness and graciousness can be fostered, which can in turn boost staff morale and positivity. For example, you could put up a note to thank a colleague for making you a cup of coffee, or another colleague who went out of their way to help you. These small good deeds add up, and make people happier to work together. It has been found that doing a kind act not only bestows a sense of satisfaction on the receiver, but also the one who performs the act, and all those who witness it.

Lastly, remembering and celebrating special days can also help foster camaraderie amongst co-workers. At SKM, we have a team of 20 and each member is an important part of the Kindness family. We organise monthly birthday celebrations and write birthday cards as a way of letting each team member know we care and appreciate them as individuals. In the same way, we multiply our joys and divide our sorrows. We believe that when we enjoy working together and have fun achieving our collective passion, we achieve a sense of well-being and become more productive. We look forward to work because we enjoy both the work and the people we work with.

Appreciation begets appreciation. Kindness begets kindness. Let it start with us.

DISCUSS

Why is appreciation at the workplace important?

What are some small ways you can show your appreciation to your team members?

Appreciate someone at work by writing him or her a thank you note and notice the difference it makes.

10

Integrating Locals and Foreigners in a Multicultural Workplace

How can organisations help staff with different backgrounds integrate and build a harmonious environment?

Singapore is an open and vibrant economy. Rooted in its Asian cultures and located at the crossroads of global trade, Singapore has fostered a multiracial and multicultural society by drawing from different cultures and ideas. This has been a competitive advantage for us.

With over 170,000 Employment Pass (EP) holders as of December 2020 – of which workers from India, China, Japan, Malaysia, the Philippines, and Britain form two-thirds – and 7,000 multinational companies operating in Singapore, we are a global workplace from people of different nationalities.[36]

The proportion of EP holders from India doubled to 25 per cent last year, from 14 per cent in 2005.[37] This was driven by the growth of Singapore's digital economy as we strive to be a technology, infrastructure development, research, and innovation hub.

Manpower Minister Tan See Leng explained that "as every sector seeks to be digitally enabled, their need for tech talent has grown significantly", emphasising that Singapore currently does not have enough locals to fill the jobs available. As of July 2021, in the Infocomm sector alone, 6,000 jobs remain unfilled.

While some Singaporeans have a concern with competition for jobs and opportunities at the workplace, most understand the economic arguments for having EP holders and appreciate a multicultural workplace.

According to an Institute of Policy Studies (IPS) survey[38] of about 4,000 Singapore citizens and permanent residents in 2020, nine in 10 of those surveyed felt that it was good to have people of different nationalities living in the same neighbourhood. They also said they could learn a lot from the immigrants' cultures.

Likewise, businesses stand to gain when their employees from different backgrounds work and interact well at the workplace. Inclusive and harmonious workplaces tend to have more engaged employees, with more innovative teams that are better at solving problems and creating value. They can better attract and retain talent, and are likely to be more productive.

Companies have realised that a talent pool made up of a hybrid of local and foreign staff needs to be able to work and coexist harmoniously in order to succeed.

But this is easier said than done. What can organisations do to help staff with different backgrounds integrate in the workplace and build a harmonious environment?

Help New Foreign Employees Adapt to Local Workplaces and Local Culture

A well-structured onboarding programme will provide a good start to a strong relationship between employer and employee, and a useful introduction to the norms, values, and culture of an organisation.

Specifically for new foreign employees, employers can share about Singapore's socio-cultural norms, so that they can learn and adapt to Singapore's values, cultures, and norms. Employers can also assign local employees to buddy up with new foreign hires to help them settle in more quickly.

Additionally, employers can take the initiative to be more aware of cultural backgrounds, values, and interests of employees. Building relationships through increased understanding and trust helps to foster inclusion.

Employers can take advantage of such knowledge to meet specific needs of employees, and make them feel more welcome.

Create Opportunities for Employees to Interact and Forge Bonds

Employers can also organise bonding activities for employees. This can include Corporate Social Responsibility initiatives that allow employees to contribute to a common good together.

Activities to develop cross-cultural understanding and competencies amongst employees can be part of staff development programmes. Employers can encourage new foreign employees to join external interest groups and to participate in activities with locals, such as networking sessions in professional associations.

As working from home becomes part of the new normal, it may be more difficult to meet in person, but there are ways to help remote teams thrive, such as organising regular video conferences to update each other about our lives, or catching up physically over a meal in small groups.

Eliminating Bias

Lastly, it is important to ensure all employees feel they are getting equal opportunities. Internally, performance and reward metrics should ideally be built on the same basis for everyone, irrespective of origin and background of staff. Practising fairness will avoid any anti-foreigner sentiment that may create an "us versus them" mentality.

Additionally, when considering employees for promotion, companies should take the best-fit approach, seeking the best person for the job based on merit and skill sets, without regard to whether they are local or foreign.

While there are challenges to workplace integration, we need to remain open in order for businesses to thrive and succeed through the pandemic and beyond.

Said Minister for Culture, Community, and Youth Edwin Tong in July 2021: "I find that it's important that we don't just talk about integration, but we make it a lived experience daily."

DISCUSS

What are the benefits of a multicultural workplace?

What is your organisation doing to encourage workplace integration?

What more can be done?

11

Your Daily Job Can Make a Difference to Others

Through one act of kindness, be it at home or at our workplace, we can create a kind, gracious society.

There is a story about four people named Everybody, Somebody, Anybody, and Nobody. A very important task had to be accomplished and Everybody was sure that Somebody would do it. Anybody could have done it but Nobody did it. Somebody got very angry about this because it was Everybody's job. Everybody thought Anybody could do it, but Nobody realised that Everybody wouldn't do it.

The 17th-century French playwright Molière once said: "It is not only for what we do that we are held responsible, but also for what we do not do."

What we do is generally understood by all. It is what we do not do, thinking that it is not our individual responsibility, that is often a problem.

We are responsible for how we treat others. Whether we are in a private, government, or non-profit organisation, we have the power and responsibility to make a difference in our workplace, and to the community around us, by doing good beyond our call of duty.

We can reach out to one another by simply asking "How are you today?" and then providing a listening ear. We can even challenge ourselves to do one random act of kindness every day, be it opening the door for others, offering a cup of coffee to a colleague, or inviting a new colleague out for lunch.

We can also pay it forward with Corporate Social Responsibility (CSR) programmes and collective acts of kindness. CSR is the way we make the business of kindness our business beyond generating profits. The benefits of kindness have the power to transform an organisation to not only enrich the lives of its employees, but also the community it operates in.

CSR is about giving back to the community, and it starts with being aware of what the community needs. It is about serving others through volunteering our time and effort, or simply performing small acts of kindness for the people we meet daily.

Many studies have shown that doing good deeds for others leads to happier people. Helping others bestows a sense of satisfaction on the receiver, the giver, and all who witnessed the kind act. When we help others, our brains release a mixture of chemicals, including dopamine, which makes us feel good.[39] Hence, by being kind, we influence others to be kind too, and this produces an endless chain of effects, a virtuous circle of kindness.

Dr Martin Luther King, Jr once said: "Life's most persistent and urgent question is, what are you doing for others?" As an organisation, we need to ask, what are we doing for others that is making a positive difference? And more importantly, as an individual, what am I doing to serve others in my workplace and community?

In 2014, the Singapore Kindness Movement partnered with Gardenia in a month-long campaign to encourage acts of kindness in daily life. For each hashtag #NationofKindness on social media, SKM donated a loaf of Gardenia bread to families in need. A total of more than 4,900 loaves of bread were distributed.

As part of our team-building activities, we also volunteer with various charity organisations such as The Volunteer Switchboard and Waterways Watch Society to help in the good work they do.

A kind and gracious society starts with each one of us making a difference in our workplaces, homes, and the spaces we interact in. It all starts with one act of kindness at a time.

DISCUSS

How are you making a difference to others in your workplace and community?

CSR is about giving back to the community. What is one group of people in your community you can serve?

For your next team bonding activity, choose to volunteer your time and effort to help the less fortunate.

12

Support Local Artists Within Our Community

Both corporates and individuals can play a part in supporting local artists.

The arts scene in Singapore has undoubtedly become more vibrant. More Singaporeans are appreciating the arts, whether visual, performing, or literary. According to the Ministry of

Culture, Community and Youth (MCCY), attendance at arts and culture events hit a record 13.6 million in 2018.

It is encouraging to see a crescendo of fresh voices on the arts scene. SingLit festivals and Singaporeans bagging prestigious international awards are good signs that people are starting to pay attention.

The arts help us to broaden our perspectives, enrich our lives, and bring people together. Not only that, art plays an important role in promoting culture and strengthening our national identity.

Singapore's arts scene also contributes to a more inclusive society. Special-needs artists have painted murals to brighten our city. Migrant workers have penned stories and poems, and published books launched at Singapore's first migrant literature festival in December 2019.

Initiatives such as Arts in Your Neighbourhood, Art Reach, and Silver Art focus on bringing the arts to Singaporeans of all ages and from all walks of life, including seniors and low-income families.

By engaging with the arts, individuals in our workforce and communities will have opportunities to nurture empathy and be stirred to explore their own creative abilities. It builds the next generation of all-rounded and innovative thinkers and provides alternative voices to help shape the future of the country.

Yet it remains difficult for Singaporeans to pursue artistic careers full-time and sustain themselves financially. Some have to work odd jobs to supplement their income. This, despite government efforts to increase public participation in the arts, better technology in making art accessible and a more appreciative public.

Why is that?

There are a number of reasons. Foremost is the mindset of Singaporeans. Many parents still do not encourage their children to pursue the arts as a vocation, perceiving it as a "dead-end" career with little material reward, a few outstanding ones exempted.

Take buskers, for example. They continue to be stigmatised by some as people who cannot find a "real" job. Yet many do so out of a passion to share their music with the public.

Something within the Singaporean psyche appears to condition many of us to believe that local art is of lesser value than art from overseas. Greater recognition and appreciation is often accorded to international artists. This bias can be seen in Singaporean artists often being deemed as "struggling" until they "make it" on the international stage.

But there are encouraging signs. Corporate support provides the lifeline for many local artists.

United Overseas Bank Limited (UOB) has championed art in Singapore through its flagship competition, the UOB Painting of the Year, and through a range of outreach initiatives. UOB also supports visual arts programmes at Pathlight School, Northlight School, and Little Arts Academy, which enable children with special needs and underprivileged children to receive quality education in the arts and help them better integrate into society.

JCDecaux Singapore sponsored media spaces at bus shelters to promote local arts events, and Orchard Turn Developments offered space to homegrown artists to showcase their work at Ion Orchard shopping mall.

In July 2019, SKM and Raffles City Singapore launched an

exhibition featuring 200 40cm-tall Singa the Lion figurines hand-painted by individuals, including President Halimah Yacob. The exhibition brought together members of the local community to share their Singapore stories and visions on kindness. The campaign raised S$300,000, which benefited six charities under the President's Challenge 2019.

In 2019, *The Straits Times* reported that donations to Singapore's arts and cultural scene rose for the first time in three years, with in-kind giving at an all-time high of S$24.5 million. These funds enable arts organisations and professionals to hone their craft and flourish, ensuring our arts ecosystem gets the continuity and sustainability it needs.

Individuals can also play their part by donating or contributing their time, passion, and skills to the arts.

Charity begins at home. Kindness must start within our own community. To encourage local works and appreciate local talents, we need to change our mindset and believe that local art can be just as evocative, important, and valuable as that created overseas.

By supporting local artists, we can create a more vibrant and inclusive community with a shared understanding and appreciation of our uniquely Singapore culture.

DISCUSS

When was the last time you attended an arts event in Singapore? What did you take away from it?

Do you think the arts encourages a more inclusive society? Why or why not?

How can you or your organisation better support the arts scene?

13

Appreciate Delivery Riders More to Support the Gig Economy

When we think of frontline heroes in the fight against Covid-19, let's not forget our delivery riders.

When we think of frontline heroes, we think of doctors and nurses who have been working around the clock to care for the sick among us in the never-ending Covid-19 fight.

We also think of the cleaners who disinfect our public areas to keep our community safe from the virus. Yet we often forget another about group of frontline heroes: our delivery riders.

During Phase Two (Heightened Alert), stricter measures such as no dining-in and a return to work-from-home (WFH) as the norm were put in place. That meant that the majority of Singaporeans had to swap eating out for takeaway and food delivery.

Unlike many of us, delivery riders, as well as many others in the gig economy, cannot work from home. They have to brave the elements and Covid-19 risks to keep our nation running.

A delivery driver, Jarrold Tham, recently admitted to the media that right now, he hardly makes $100 a week from deliveries as compared to the $70–100 per day during peak periods in 2020.

It seems that unlike the 2020 Circuit Breaker, even though online orders have increased, delivery riders like him have not seen an increase in income.

According to *TODAY*,[40] only one out of nine delivery riders reported a slight rise in earnings. This could be due to more of them working this period – private-hire drivers are also picking up food deliveries to supplement a drop in their earnings – thus the earnings are spread even thinner.

Being a food delivery rider during this time is not an easy job – they are constantly on the go, even to the extent of eating meals by the roadside, in order to put food on the table. Thankfully, some groups have taken the initiative to set up rest areas for delivery riders to eat and rest.

Nevertheless, it is still a stressful, thankless job.

In May 2021, the wife of a delivery rider who died while delivering goods had to respond to text messages from impatient customers asking about their goods despite just finding out that her husband had passed away. She later shared about the challenges facing delivery riders and asked for more empathy from both customers, and the organisations that employ these gig workers.[41]

It's easy for us to feel entitled, especially when we (organisations or customers) are paying for a service. While it is okay to expect some level of professionalism, let's remember that the people performing the service are human too, just like us.

So beyond just giving them a five-star review, let's give them a little extra appreciation and support.

I am glad that Singaporeans have been playing our part.

Contribute.sg, a ground-up movement supported by the Singapore Kindness Movement, is working with Sengkang Community Club and IllustrateSG to make appreciation cards for food delivery riders in the Sengkang area in June 2021.

Children from kindergartens will colour these appreciation cards, part of an appreciation pack (including surgical mask and UV-protection arm sleeves) to show our gratitude to delivery riders.

Singaporeans are also reaching out on their own to encourage delivery riders. In several instances, customers have ordered meals, not to deliver to their own addresses, but for riders to share among themselves. Many more have tipped their riders – done through the delivery apps – as a small token of appreciation.

For my birthday, which happened to fall during the Heightened Alert (HA) period, I arranged for a box of my favourite kueh to be delivered to each of my staff and council members. It was a small token to thank all of them for their hard work and to support the hawkers and the delivery riders at the same time.

The gig economy will continue to grow as more organisations digitalise and more people buy their food and other essentials via apps.

It is also important for employers to protect the rights and interests of their workers, whether it be offering better rewards and benefits or stronger protection and safety nets.

Now, when these gig economy workers are faced with more uncertainty and lower incomes, our personal gestures of support can be a meaningful and impactful way to say thank you.

When we think of frontline heroes in the fight against Covid-19, let's not forget about what delivery riders do.

For all their hard work, the least we can do the next time we order a meal is to give them a big smile and thank them, and leave a tip if you can!

DISCUSS

How has the pandemic affected those working in the gig economy?

How can organisations support and protect the rights and interests of their gig workers?

How can you show your support and appreciation for frontline workers such as delivery riders?

14

Don't Let Black Sheep Prevent Good Deeds

Can we still be kind amid scams and fake news?

Scams are becoming more prevalent and deceptive. Channel NewsAsia reported that crime went up seven per cent in the first half of 2019, mainly due to a rise in scam cases. E-commerce, loan, credit-for-sex, and Internet love scams collectively make up 80 per cent of the top 10 scam types.[42] The total number of reported cases for these four types of scams increased by more than 1,000 – almost 60 per cent – compared to the same period in 2018.

In particular, scammers have been using digital platforms such as Facebook, Carousell, and Lazada to extend their reach.

In November 2019, a bogus report masquerading as one by *The Straits Times* falsely quoted Temasek Holdings CEO Ho Ching urging Singaporeans "to jump on (an) amazing opportunity before the big banks shut it down for good", referring to an investment scheme that claimed to make "hundreds of people in Singapore very rich".[43]

Such fake articles promoted by fake ads on Facebook have been circulating for months.

Why do people fall prey to such scams?

There is often an assumption that the victims are elderly, less educated, or socially isolated, and thus more vulnerable to being conned.

But there is no basis for this assumption. No one is immune to fraud. Sometimes, people simply fall for scams due to the psychological techniques used by scammers.

Scams don't prey on people; they prey on people's emotions. Often, the offer guarantees that you will win money or get rich quick. This appeal to greed overrides natural caution.

Fear is another tactic. In September 2019, a 21-year-old Chinese national was accused by a "police officer" of being involved in a money laundering scheme. Desperate to clear her name, she did what she was told and transferred a total of S$500,000 to the scammers.

Riding on the authority of government entities such as the police, or in Ms Ho Ching's case, the credibility of personalities in Singapore, these scams fool the public into putting money into bogus schemes.

But in my opinion, the worst scammers prey on the kindness of people.

There has been a wave of fake online fundraising campaigns on Facebook. The pattern is familiar: scammers post emotive stories, usually about terminally ill children who need money for immediate medical treatment.

Many are taken in by the plight of the children and donate. Unfortunately, failing to verify the truth of the situation, they end up transferring money to scammers instead.

So here is our challenge. Can we still be kind despite this danger of being cheated?

Yes, we can and we should. There are real people in real circumstances who need our help. Many families in Singapore continue to struggle in one- and two-room rental flats, and rely on food donation programmes for meals.

Scams have always existed. The Internet has made them more pervasive. But the Internet can be used for good, too.

After *The Pride* shared the story of 5-year-old boy Haiqel, who was born in jail and had never celebrated his birthday, there was overwhelming support for Haiqel's aunt and guardian, Ms Suhaini Md Ali, and Ms Janice Yap, a single mother who sponsored a birthday celebration for him. A flurry of messages showing support and showering praise on both Ms Suhaini and Ms Yap were left in the Facebook comments section. Some even offered to buy groceries for Ms Suhaini's family and toys for Haiqel.

In another story, local volunteer group It's Raining Raincoats raised S$158,000 in public donations for the family of foreign worker, Mr Velmurugan Muthian, who was killed in a crane collapse in November.

Social media can exacerbate fake news and scams, but it can also bring awareness and help – in cash or kind – much closer and faster to those in need.

We need to be careful in differentiating scammers from genuine people and charitable organisations.

Charity organisations usually do not resort to strong emotive appeals, because it is more important for them to build trusting relationships with donors.

Most are also required to report how they spend the money they receive as a measure of accountability.

To ensure that your money goes where it is intended, donate to a known foundation unless you are sure the individual or group is trustworthy.

If you are able, volunteering your time to a cause can be a meaningful experience to help others in need.

How about participating in your organisation's corporate social responsibility (CSR) programmes? You can even take the initiative to organise a volunteer event as part of team-bonding.

A study on employees who actively participate in CSR initiatives found that helping others sparked a sense of compassion and generosity in the volunteers themselves. As a result, participants experienced a progressive change within themselves that evoked a feeling of fulfilment, and ultimately joy.[44]

The Internet has increased our ability to show kindness to others. We should not let the acts of a few black sheep prevent us from doing good.

DISCUSS

Do online scams and fake news make you more wary to donate?

How can you differentiate scammers from genuine people and charitable organisations?

How can you or your organisation use social media for good?

15

Humanising the Modern Workplace

When people are valued before profits, they become much more productive, and profits come naturally.

The disruptive culture brought on by technological innovations escalates the level of business competition: the more technologically integrated a business is, the greater its focus on the bottom-line. It is more challenging today to cultivate a genuine human connection at work.

Singapore employees are the least engaged among major Asian markets, as reported in 2018, with employee engagement levels at 59 per cent, compared to the Asia-Pacific average of 65 per cent.[45]

Studies show that in order to thrive in the modern workplace, organisations need to build a healthy, human environment where its people can grow. Part of creating a more human workplace is getting to know employees as complete people with goals, families, and interests. Human workplaces give priority to ideals like high-quality relationships, trust-building, and personal and professional growth.

When leaders take the time to translate these ideals into practice, a deeper bond and transformation is forged in the workplace.

Is Technology Killing Human Connectivity?

Technology has undeniably made us more connected than ever and revolutionised the way we work. However, all that hyper-connectivity has ironically made us less communicative: just think of office exchanges, self-checkout counters, and online purchases. Interpersonal interactions have been replaced by screens. We sit at our desks typing emails trying to resolve problems through technology, when we could easily (and more effectively) walk over to a colleague for a face-to-face discussion.

While technology is harnessed to enable people to be more productive, efficient, and innovative, it must not undermine people's need to feel safe and cared for and remain internally and externally connected. Technology should instead facilitate the comfortable and expeditious flow of people, emotions, and ideas. Ultimately, it is still just a tool. On its own, technology does not have the power to make us feel less or more human. That is up to us.

Create a Safe Space for Employees to Bond

One way to build a more human workplace is to provide opportunities for bonding within and across teams. Research suggests that playing and eating together are good ways to foster cooperation. Companies like Google and Facebook organise shared games, sports, exercise, and meals while LinkedIn has encouraged employees to take their personal lives to work by hosting "Bring in Your Parents Day".

Intentionally getting to know co-workers as friends can give us a sense of belonging and help pull us through the day-to-day challenges of work and life.

Professor Jane E. Dutton from the University of Michigan finds that a high-quality connection does not require "a deep or intimate relationship". A single interaction marked by respect, trust, and mutual engagement is enough to generate energy for both parties. However small they appear, those moments of connection can transform a transaction into a relationship.

People Before Profits

It goes without saying that profits are important to businesses. But it is people who generate profits. Therefore, people must come before profits, and profits follow productive people.

When an organisation invests in its people, and shows kindness to them, employees will reciprocate with a sense of loyalty that is authentic. It is therefore important to cultivate individual strengths and treat each individual as a valued member of the organisation. Giving constructive feedback, mentoring, and coaching team members are indications that people are genuinely cared for. Leaders should take the time to reach out to their people when good things happen, not just when something goes wrong.

A simple "thank you", "good job", or even making time to stop by an employee's desk to speak to them face-to-face can help close the communication gap and empower employees to perform better in their roles. It allows them to feel that their hard work and sacrifices are valued.

Indeed, kindness goes beyond the pursuit of wealth and economic value. When we become less transactional and more relational, setting one another up for success, we discover that kindness humanises the technologically wired workplace. It transforms a cold, ordinary workplace into a warm, human workplace.

In that kind of space, people will be more willing to invest in their work, innovate new ideas, and go the extra mile for the organisation. Where people are valued before profits, they become much more productive, and profits come naturally.

DISCUSS

Do you think technology has enhanced or disrupted human connection?

Think about your relationships with your colleagues. Would you say they are more transactional or relational?

How can an organisation invest in its people?

16

Where Is Kindness in the Digital Age?

Organisations that can strike a balance between creating a supportive, gracious environment where workers thrive, while tackling new technology and innovations, will ultimately succeed in the long run.

With increased automation in businesses today, we are seeing the rise of self-checkout counters, chatbots, and online purchases. Interactions that were once between people are now redirected toward screens. Even fast-food restaurants like McDonald's have introduced digital self-order kiosks which will soon be available at all 14,000 McDonald's outlets in the United States.

Technology is advancing relentlessly and the sci-fi vision of automation replacing people causing massive loss of lower-level jobs is already happening. Thanks to artificial intelligence (AI), machines can now not only carry out mundane manual labour, but also perform some cognitive tasks.

Scientists even predict that, in the foreseeable future, they will be able to develop a robot equivalent of a chief executive officer (CEO) that can write and deliver speeches and even serve on boards and make complex decisions.[46]

However, while machines can perform given tasks, often more efficiently than humans, they lack the uniquely human ability to cater to the emotional and psychological needs of the individual (for now, at least). For that reason, there are many of us who still prefer to be served by a feeling and empathetic human.

This is especially true in the healthcare industry. Machines may be able to diagnose and even treat more efficiently, but many of us still feel more comfortable working with a doctor who has been trained to walk us through the options and administer the treatment protocol, one who understands our fears and emotions. The traits of kindness, empathy, and compassion cannot be replaced.

Put the "Human" Back into Human Resource

Imagine a world where we board a driverless bus or train to work, communicate through emails and web conferences, and retreat to our individual homes at the end of the day. How cold and isolating would that be?

People still matter, especially in the workplace, where we spend the majority of our waking hours.

Human resource (HR) professionals are often mistaken for administrative staff who hire and fire, and draw up policies and guidelines for employees to adhere to.

However, HR, as its name suggests, is about valuing human capital as a precious resource. The best of HR professionals are advocates of the well-being of human beings at work. They foster a culture where people treat each other humanely with respect, compassion, and kindness. They systematically address our human need for appreciation, belonging, and opportunities to contribute in a meaningful way.

While kindness and graciousness are sometimes seen as soft values which are nice-to-have but not necessarily a priority on a company's corporate agenda, they serve a powerful role in boosting morale and camaraderie among happy and engaged workers. It is in the interest of the organisation to make kindness and graciousness a way of life in the workplace.

HR leaders who understand this dynamic can more effectively engage their employees' best talents, support collaborative teams, and create an environment that fosters productive change.

Enhance Communication with Technology

Whatever the downside of technology, there is no denying that technology has, at the same time, made us more connected than ever, and revolutionised the way we work.

Technology allows workers to stay connected internally and externally and facilitates the expeditious flow of ideas. If technology is our servant and not our master, we can take charge and improve the quality of communication between humans through the machines.

A kind and gracious way of communicating is essential for enhancing positive relationships within the workplace. Here are four ways to sustain your organisation's human touch well into the digital age[47]:

1. Encourage more staff interaction with regular staff lunches and team-bonding activities

2. Create open spaces or hot-desking opportunities for staff to work together

3. Use new technology to pair up staff as mentors

4. Gather everyone's phones into a "Talk Away Box"[48] and disconnect to reconnect with each other, paying closer attention to the conversations around the room

Achieving the balance between creating a supportive, gracious environment where workers thrive, while also tackling new technology and innovations is not going to be easy. However, organisations that reflect this ethos will ultimately succeed in the long run.

After all, an organisation is made up of people. Without the opportunity to give and receive kindness through face-to-face interactions, where would that leave us as a workforce, and more importantly, as a society?

The next time you take a coffee break, why not take the initiative to ask a colleague along? A genuine conversation and connection could be the start of an invaluable friendship. Whether in our workplaces, neighbourhoods, or homes, we all have a need to connect and build relationships.

We are social beings; the need for relationships is in our DNA.

DISCUSS

What are your thoughts on the increased automation in businesses today, with self-checkout counters, chatbots, and online purchases?

What is the role of Human Resources at your workplace?

How can we put the "human" back into Human Resources?

17

Can Excellent Customer Service Exist Without Kindness?

Bad customer service is frustrating, so be kind and make someone's day.

In our interactions with others, be it with friends, colleagues, or strangers, it is easy to recognise when we have been treated kindly or unkindly.

Similarly, we can easily distinguish good customer service from bad customer service. Good customer service usually puts a smile on our face and often makes our day. This happens when service staff understand our needs and go the extra mile to help us find the product or service that we need, or resolve a problem. Even in the case of online stores, a personalised note received in the mail makes all the difference.

On the other hand, bad customer service can make one feel frustrated and helpless.

While there are many things that can affect the retail experience of a shopper – online or offline – customer service is undoubtedly one of the top factors that impact how shoppers perceive brands.

According to the American Express 2017 Customer Service Barometer[49], 50 per cent of consumers have abandoned a purchase due to poor service experience, 70 per cent say they would spend more money with a business that provides great customer service consistently, and 33 per cent say they'd look to switch to a competitor after a single bad service experience.

What Determines Excellent Customer Service?

Those working in the retail, food and beverage (F&B), or hospitality industry would be no stranger to a list of "X steps to great customer service" in their training programmes upon starting with an organisation. Some common steps include: start with a smile, be polite and respectful, anticipate what the customer needs, respond promptly, and so on.

These steps are all important in ensuring a pleasant customer experience. However, excellent customer service requires more than following a formula or series of steps. Sustainable excellent customer service needs to come from the heart.

It is the attitude of kindness in us that allows us to empathise with the customers' needs. Approaching difficult customers with a positive attitude can completely change expectations and turn the situation around. Small acts of kindness and empathy can go a long way to make customers feel cared for and served.

The Disney brand is more than a theme park with rides; Disney sells an experience. They have captured what it means to provide customer service with kindness. In fact, it's required by "cast members," as Disney park employees are called, to make sure that customers are having a great day.[50] That might mean handing out a pin, replacing a dropped ice-cream cone, giving directions, answering every question with more than "I don't know", or just finding out why a child is crying. Each staff is empowered to embody kindness.

Embodying Kindness in Customer Service

An attitude of kindness and graciousness is only possible when it stems from a company culture of kindness. If we want our employees to treat our customers with kindness, we must treat our employees first with kindness.

Kindness is all about treating our customers and employees as people – appreciating them, getting to know them, listening to them, and showing that we care. It is no accident that The Ritz-Carlton addresses all their staff as "ladies and gentlemen".

The benefits to the organisation are plenty.

When kindness is part of the company culture, employees are more likely to work hard for the company and go the extra mile. Kindness can also boost staff morale and employee engagement. This translates to a more motivated workforce and lower staff turnover, so employers can better retain talent. Companies will find that because of their positive reputation, it will not be difficult to find top talent, as kind people are naturally attracted to kind organisations.

A culture of kindness is great for a company's brand. In a world where consumers have an abundance of brands that they can choose from, kindness can be the difference in winning customers. Genuine acts of kindness, good deeds, and selflessness – whether small or large – allow brands to stay authentic so that people can connect with them.

Actions Speak Louder Than Words

Consumers today are perceptive and can easily tell if a brand campaign is authentic or merely a public relations stunt. Hence, it is important that the customer experience needs to be aligned with the message, and that employees walk the talk.

As automation increases and more brick-and-mortar stores move online, brands need to adapt to new technologies and channels of communications. The ways in which employees interact with customers are also changing.

However, as long as a culture of kindness and graciousness exists within the organisation, and its values are at the core of all internal and external communication, I believe excellent customer service, however manifested in the new economy, will still be felt and appreciated by customers. It will not become a thing of the past.

DISCUSS

Think of an occasion when you experienced great customer service. What made you think so?

How important are kindness and the authenticity of a brand for consumers?

How can each team member be empowered to embody kindness?

18

Practising Kindness@Work in the New Normal

Covid-19 has changed the way we live and work, but we can still be kind to each other.

The Covid-19 pandemic has thrown the world into crisis.

But even before Covid, we were already living in a VUCA (Volatile, Uncertain, Complex and Ambiguous) world – a combination of qualities that characterise the chaotic world we live in.

The volatility, uncertainty, complexity and ambiguity of the pandemic has not only upended lives, but revealed ugly behaviour such as panic buying, hoarding, disputes arising from individuals flouting the rules, and even attacks on safe-distancing officers.

Employee mental health has also been pushed to the forefront as job uncertainty and isolation continue to take a toll on workers. A workplace resilience survey published in August 2020 even found that those working from home can be more stressed than those working on the front lines of the Covid-19 pandemic.[51]

But all is not gloom and doom. Kindness has also emerged within the chaos of Covid-19.

We have seen residents placing hand sanitisers in lifts to share with neighbours, individuals donating their S$600 Solidarity Payments to those who need it more, and groups coming together to appreciate front-line workers and helping the vulnerable in society.

Many Singaporeans have also said that the pandemic has given them the opportunity to look out for loved ones and appreciate them more. One silver lining of Covid-19 and working from home is that it has given us more time for the people and things that matter.

As we learn to adapt to the new normal and live in a world still reeling from Covid-19, we need a new definition of VUCA.

We need to be *vigilant* – mindful of what is happening around us and responding correctly. Vigilance is practising social responsibility and being careful – maintaining personal hygiene and keeping public spaces clean, wearing masks, and staying home when possible – so that the virus can be contained.

Where uncertainty looms, we need to be *united* – as a nation

– to overcome challenges thrown our way. Our common humanity is threatened by the virus. We are more likely to be on top of it when we are united in our social compact not only to take care of ourselves but also to take care of others.

Covid-19 has shown us that the challenges facing us are intertwined, where trade-offs, like restarting economies while containing the virus, are often a delicate balancing act.

In such a complex world, being *compassionate* – showing care and concern for each other at all times – is more important than ever.

When we internalise such values of other-centredness and empathy, we become a kinder and stronger nation, willing to give our money and time to help others, including migrant workers and lower-income households.

Lastly, in an ambiguous world, being *adaptable* – in approaching work, studies, and parenting – will be an important life skill.

We need to learn from past lessons to deal with future challenges. This allows us to thrive in the "new normal", where working from home becomes a permanent feature of our lives.

A redefined VUCA – being Vigilant, United, Compassionate and Adaptable – can guide us in practising positive values at home and in the workplace.

As we return to the office, let's continue to practise Kindness@Work in the new normal.

1. Be considerate and follow the safety measures to help everyone feel and be safe. When meeting new people, use socially distanced alternatives like the namaste or a simple bow instead of the common handshake.

2. Be empathetic to your colleagues' concerns as they may have vulnerable family members and may need longer to adjust. Check in with your teammates to find out how they are coping.

3. Adopt practical measures to take care of workers' mental well-being. The Tripartite Advisory on mental well-being at workplaces recommends appointing representatives to organise programmes, talks, and workshops on mental wellness. It also advocates training on self-care and equipping managers and human resource personnel with skills to be supportive leaders. Companies should also provide access to employee assistance programmes.

Covid-19 will be part of the new normal even as we progress to Phase 3 and beyond. However, when we show kindness to ourselves and those around us, we can have the strength and resilience to overcome as one.

DISCUSS

How has Covid-19 changed the way you work? What does the new normal in your workplace look like?

How can you show kindness to others in the new normal – in your community and workplace?

Check in with your teammate to ask how they are adjusting to the changes and coping in terms of mental health.

19

Trust and Communication Help Remote Teams Thrive

The success of remote work depends on mutual trust and open communication between employees and employers.

Working from home (WFH) is part of the new normal. Even before Circuit Breaker measures were implemented from April 2020, many organisations, SKM included, had already started telecommuting.

Despite having started WFH arrangements in advance, the shift to full-time remote work posed several challenges for our 20-strong team.

First, there was a drop in interpersonal contact. In an office environment, there are many subtle interactions that go unnoticed – a kind word, a shared joke, a passing comment – that help build relationships. Now that all our meetings are scheduled and on screens, that interactivity is gone.

While technology still enables us to meet virtually, face-to-face communication is still more effective, especially when building relationships is key to our work.

Second, home-based learning (HBL) means that parents now have to juggle work and caring for children at home. This is especially difficult for staff with young children, who have to accommodate their schedules to work productively.

Both these factors, a reduction of face-to-face interactions and an increase in home distractions, have made it a challenge to encourage synergy and kinship – core values of SKM.

Experts have predicted that working from home may be the future, even after Covid-19 fades. Companies are becoming more flexible in employees' work arrangements, allowing staggered hours and telecommuting, for example – and Covid-19 has accelerated this transition.

Mutual Trust and Understanding

However, the success of remote work depends heavily on mutual trust and understanding between employees and employers.

In Stephen Covey's book *The Speed of Trust: The One Thing that Changes Everything*, he argues that trust increases speed and thus lowers costs in businesses. It is especially important for businesses to cultivate societal trust by contributing to the public sphere, he says.

But before cultivating trust outside the organisation, we first have to trust those within. And in this challenging situation, we need to trust that our staff will do what it takes to deliver.

Trust governs how people work together, listen to one another, and build relationships. When there is trust, collaboration and knowledge sharing is high, communication flows easily, and there is a sense of shared purpose and commitment.

On the other hand, when trust is lacking, cynicism grows, micromanagement creeps in, conflict abounds, leading to low morale and poor results.

Communicate Openly and Regularly

To build trust, we need to communicate openly and regularly. With everyone working in isolation, it is easy to give insufficient context for teammates to understand what you need. Keeping teammates in the loop helps to prevent misunderstandings.

Have regular video conferences to update each other about projects or to catch up. Don't just talk shop. Ask how others are feeling and share your feelings as well.

Video calls, as opposed to voice calls, give the added benefit of body language cues and facial expressions – not to mention interesting glimpses into your colleagues' homes! This small but cosy touch can help team members connect on a more personal level.

During the Circuit Breaker, I initiated an SKM family telemeet to check in and find out how everyone was doing. It was good to see teammates sharing about how they had adjusted to working from home – some set up makeshift workspaces, others created a board to remind them of daily tasks. We didn't just talk about work, we shared about our experiences and thoughts on Covid-19, and how each of us, in our own ways, could spread kindness in this pandemic.

Foster inclusivity. Being "in the know" makes team members feel valued and included. It can be easy for cliques to form among departments. Ensure a common source of knowledge – shared drives and meeting notes help keep communication and knowledge lines transparent.

Set Clear Goals

Be it leading a team, delegating a task, or working with colleagues on a shared goal, it is important to be clear from the get-go on the deliverables – why they are important, the timelines, budget, and other specifications.

Having clearly agreed-upon goals paves the way for building trust because it gives employees the freedom and autonomy to work out how best to deliver. At the same time, it allows you (as a manager or leader) to check in to see if they need any help. This approach helps develop responsibility, integrity, and creativity within your team.

Where there is trust and good communication, professional competence and personal character come together. This allows us to develop confidence in each other to follow through on our intentions.

Be Kind

While all of us adjust to remote work while dealing with a pandemic in our own unique living situations, let's be kind to ourselves and our staff members. Show understanding, and you will realise that employees reciprocate this kindness by delivering on their tasks, even going the extra mile for you and the organisation to achieve better results.

DISCUSS

What are some benefits of WFH?

Are you more or less productive when working from home?

How can you continue to connect with team members with less face-to-face interaction while safe distancing?

20

Mental Health in the New Workplace Normal

How can companies help employees improve mental wellness to stay healthy and productive at work?

Mental health in workplaces has been pushed to the forefront as a result of Covid-19. The uncertainty created by the pandemic and increased isolation due to working from home (WFH) have brought new challenges for everyone in the workforce.

Employees who work from home often find themselves working around the clock to signal their commitment and productivity. The resultant blurring of boundaries between work and home results in work stress and fatigue.

A workplace resilience survey conducted in May–June 2020 found that those working from home can be more stressed than those working on the front lines of the Covid-19 pandemic, due to the juggling of multiple domestic responsibilities.

With these changes and challenges, how can employees maintain healthy boundaries between work and home, and improve their mental wellness in order to stay productive at work?

And how can leaders and business owners engage and communicate effectively with staff – and colleagues with each other – while adhering to safe distancing measures?

1. Support a More Hybrid Workforce

Firstly, companies can support a more hybrid workforce by finding out the needs of their staff.

This includes supporting staff with the right infrastructure and ergonomics at home, and being more empathetic to each unique family situation. The key is striking the right balance with flexibility.

The past year has shown that people can be just as productive and experience better work-life balance when working remotely.

As we transition from WFH back to the office, or some hybrid of the two, supervisors could take a more understanding view to allow staff to travel at off-peak periods to reduce risks.

Some workers may be more anxious about being back in the office as they have vulnerable family members while others may take longer to readjust after so many months of working from home.

2. Walk the Talk

As leaders, we should provide our staff with opportunities to talk openly about their mental health and to provide the support they may need. We need to continue to lift the stigma on mental health issues by having a management team who walks the talk.

Former Nominated MP Anthea Ong told *The Straits Times*: "Leaders need to set the tone for inculcating employee well-being throughout the organisation. How leaders relate to mental health issues, what expectations they create, and whether they are able to view their employees as whole persons, influence the employee's experience at work."

In November 2020, the Tripartite Advisory on Mental Well-being at Workplaces was released.

While these guidelines are a good starting point, they are only effective when companies build mental health into the new normal of leadership, to transform the culture of stigma to acceptance and inclusion.

For example, leaders can create opportunities for conversations in a one-on-one setting as some may not be comfortable speaking up about their problems in a group setting. Empathy and compassion from a manager can go a long way in providing a safe space for employees.

3. Look Out for Signs and Reach Out

We can also look out for signs of mental health issues in ourselves and our colleagues.

At work, we might notice that we are more tired than usual. We might make uncharacteristic mistakes or find it hard to motivate ourselves. We might isolate ourselves and avoid colleagues.

We may find these early warning signs hard to see in ourselves, and it can help to have colleagues who can help us connect this to our mental health.

But how can we tell when a colleague is stressed out, especially when we can't meet face-to-face while WFH?

We can be mindful of behavioural changes, such as when a colleague who used to be very cheerful and engaged suddenly becomes withdrawn and quiet. We can also check in with our team mates regularly to ask "How are you?".

Although many aspects of our working lives have changed, there are still opportunities to connect with each other. For example, a virtual lunch over a video call.

At SKM, we continue to celebrate monthly birthdays where the team organises fun activities over Zoom. We also hold small group gatherings in split teams across departments so team members can physically catch up with one another.

Other tips for encouraging well-being and protecting mental health are exercising regularly and going outdoors, even if it's for a short walk.

It's time we see mental health as just as important as physical health so that we can be a strong and healthy workforce, even while safe distancing.

DISCUSS

What are some challenges you have experienced while WFH?

What are some signs of mental health issues such as stress and burnout that you can look out for in yourself and your colleagues?

How can you maintain healthy boundaries between work and home while WFH?

References

[1] Hamilton, D., 2011, "5 beneficial side effects of kindness", *The Huffington Post*, http://www.huffingtonpost.com/david-r-hamilton-phd/kindness-benefits_b_869537.html

[2] Connecting Happiness and Success, "Increasing productivity and profitability with happiness", http://connectinghappinessandsuccess.com/other-happiness/happiness-at-work/increasing-productivityand-profitability-with-happiness/

[3] Hall, A., 2015, "The key to happiness at work that has nothing to do with your actual job", http://www.huffingtonpost.com/2015/02/04/happiness-at-work_n_6613358.html

[4] Hartung, R., *Changing Lanes, Changing Lives* (Candid Creation Publishing, 2016); and Ronald Tay, *Leadership Conversations* (Marshall Cavendish, 2015).

[5] Fredrickson, B.L., 17 August 2004, "The broaden-and-build theory of positive emotions", The Royal Society, http://www.ncbi.nlm.nih.gov/pmc/articles/PMC1693418/pdf/15347528.pdf

[6] Carsrud, A.L., and Brännback, M. (editors), *Understanding the Entrepreneurial Mind: Opening the Black Box* (International Studies in Entrepreneurship, Volume 24, 2009).

[7] Tay, J., 2017, "Survey Results: Nearly one-quarter of Singapore workers feel bullied at work", JobsCentral, http://community.jobscentral.com.sg/articles/survey-results-nearly-one-quarter-singapore-workers-feel-bullied-work

[8] Wan, W., "Why a little kindness can improve your work", https://www.challenge.gov.sg/print/insiders-take/why-a-little-kindness-can-improve-your-work

[9] Co.tribute, "How to build camaraderie in the workplace", http://info.cotribute.com/blog/how-to-build-camaraderie-in-the-workplace

[10] Gallup, "70% of US workers not engaged at work", http://www.gallup.com/strategicconsulting/163007/state-american-workplace.aspx

[11] Dixon, A., 6 September 2011, "Kindness makes you happy... and happiness makes you kind", http://greatergood.berkeley.edu/article/item/kindness_makes_you_happy_and_happiness_makes_you_kind.

References

[12] Advani, P., 11 August 2013, "How random acts of kindness can benefit your health", http://www.huffingtonpost.com/priya-advani/random-acts-of-kindness_b_3412718.html.

[13] Siow, L.S., 27 August 2016, "S'pore workplace stress on the rise: Survey", *The Business Times*, accessed via http://www.businesstimes.com.sg/government-economy/spore-workplace-stress-on-the-rise-survey.

[14] Donvito, T., "12 surprisingly powerful health benefits of being nicer to yourself", *Reader's Digest*, accessed via https://www.rd.com/health/wellness/being-kind-to-yourself/

[15] Burton, V., March 2013, "4 things resilient people do", accessed via https://valorieburton.com/2013/03/4-things-resilient-people-do/.

[16] Seppala, E., 18 March 2015, "Positive teams are more productive", accessed via https://hbr.org/2015/03/positive-teams-are-more-productive

[17] Baker, W.F., O'Malley, M., 2008, *Leading with Kindness: How Good People Consistently Get Superior Results* (AMACOM, 2008).

[18] Kerpen, C., 18 November 2013, "Kindness does not equate to weakness in leadership", *Forbes*, https://www.forbes.com/sites/carriekerpen/2013/11/18/kindness-does-not-equate-to-weakness-in-leadership/#60efd09a42b9

[19] Nieuwhof, C., "3 hard but powerful truths about likeability and leadership", https://careynieuwhof.com/3-hard-powerful-truths-likeability-leadership/

[20] Common Sense Leadership, "About John Keyser", http://www.commonsense-leadership.com/about/

[21] Bosworth, J., 4 January 2018, "Lead with kindness: You'll get better results", http://www.incourageleading.com/lead-with-kindness-youll-get-better-results/.

[22] Cuddy, A.J.C., Kohut, M., and Neffinger, J., July–August 2013, "Connect, then lead", *Harvard Business Review*, https://hbr.org/2013/07/connect-then-lead

[23] Co.tribute, "How to build camaraderie in the workplace", http://info.cotribute.com/blog/how-to-build-camaraderie-in-the-workplace

[24] Gallup, "State of the American workplace", http://www.gallup.com/strategic-consulting/163007/state-american-workplace.aspx

[25] Levine, L., 25 June 2014, "Reasons why workplace camaraderie matters", http://hr.sparkhire.com/employee-engagement/reasons-why-workplace-camaraderie-matters/

[26] Riordan, C.M., 3 July 2013, "We all need friends at work", https://hbr.org/2013/07/we-all-need-friends-at-work

[27] Robinson, S.F., 2016, "What's in a thank you? Building a culture of appreciation", *Huffington Post*, http://www.huffingtonpost.com/sarah-finnie-robinson/

whats-in-a-thank-you-buil_b_9385666.html

[28] Tanner, O.C., 2017, "The psychological effects of workplace appreciation and gratitude", *Emergenetics International*, https://www.emergenetics.com/blog/workplace-appreciation-gratitude/

[29] Ibid.

[30] Emmons, R., *Gratitude Works!: A 21-Day Program for Creating Emotional Prosperity* (Wiley, 2013).

[31] Hartung, R., *Changing Lanes, Changing Lives* (Candid Creation Publishing, 2016); and Ronald Tay, *Leadership Conversations* (Marshall Cavendish, 2015).

[32] Buote, V., 2017, "Gratitude at work: Its impact on job satisfaction and sense of community", *Plasticity Labs*.

[33] Cornerstone, 2017, "Survey reveals Americans don't feel valued in the workplace – and employers are overlooking simple solutions", https://www.cornerstoneondemand.com/2010-4-29+Survey+Reveals+Americans+Don%E2%80%99t+Feel+Valued+in+the+Workplace+%E2%80%93+and+Employers+are+Overlooking+Simple+Solutions

[34] Smith, M.W., 6 August 2014, "Workplace appreciation can be pretty simple – and effective", *TLNT*, https://www.eremedia.com/tlnt/workplace-appreciation-it-can-be-pretty-simple-and-effective/

[35] Forbes, 13 September 2007, "Why is it so hard to say 'well done'?", https://www.forbes.com/2007/09/13/workplace-careers-recognition-lead-careers-cx_mk_0913robbins.html

[36] Ministry of Manpower, "Foreign workforce numbers", accessed via https://www.mom.gov.sg/documents-and-publications/foreign-workforce-numbers

[37] Yang, C., 8 July 2021, *The Straits Times*, "Indian EP holders nearly doubled to 25%, driven by digital economy growth", accessed via https://www.straitstimes.com/singapore/politics/proportion-of-indian-ep-holders-doubled-but-not-a-result-of-more-favourable

[38] Yap, J., 3 August 2019, *CNA*, "More than 6 in 10 feel immigrants not doing enough to integrate into Singapore: Survey", accessed via https://www.channelnewsasia.com/singapore/more-6-10-feel-immigrants-not-doing-enough-integrate-singapore-survey-862641

[39] Hamilton, D.R., 2011, "5 beneficial side effects of kindness", *The Huffington Post*, http://www.huffingtonpost.com/david-r-hamilton-phd/kindness-benefits_b_869537.html

[40] Ong, J., 19 May 2021, *TODAY*, "Covid-19: With no dining in, food delivery firms report jump in demand but some riders see little change in earnings", accessed via https://www.todayonline.com/singapore/covid-19-no-dining-

food-delivery-firms-report-jump-demand-some-riders-see-little-change

[41] Teo, R., 25 May 2021, *The Pride*, "Her husband died while delivering goods, but she still wanted to show kindness to his customers", accessed via https://pride.kindness.sg/husband-died-delivering-goods/

[42] 30 August 2019, *CNA*, "Crime up 7% in first half of 2019, mainly due to rise in scam cases: Police", accessed via https://www.channelnewsasia.com/news/singapore/crime-up-first-half-of-2019-rise-in-scam-cases-11856622

[43] Yong, C., *The Straits Times*, "Ho Ching warns against scam ads that 'make up fake breathtaking quotes from me'", accessed via https://www.straitstimes.com/singapore/fat-frogs-jumping-in-the-streets-ho-ching-warns-of-fake-reports-using-her-name-to-trick

[44] April 2018, "The experiences of employees participating in organisational corporate social responsibility initiatives", *Research Gate*, accessed via https://www.researchgate.net/publication/324544995_The_experiences_of_employees_participating_in_organisational_corporate_social_responsibility_initiatives

[45] Media OutReach, 28 March 2018, "2018 Employee engagement trends: Singapore employees least engaged among major Asian markets", *Business Insider Singapore*, https://www.businessinsider.sg/2018-employee-engagement-trends-singapore-employees-leastengaged-among-major-asian-markets/

[46] Finkel, A., August 2017, "Robots won't replace us because we still need the human touch", *Cosmos*, https://cosmosmagazine.com/society/robots-won-t-replace-us-because-we-still-need-that-human-touch

[47] HRD, 15 August 2017, "Six ways to keep a human touch in an automating world", *Human Resources Director*, https://www.hcamag.com/hr-news/six-ways-to-keep-a-human-touch-in-an-automatingworld-239958.aspx

[48] SKM created a "Talk Away Box" to keep all the mobile phones during a meeting. They are available on request by the HR department.

[49] Ciotti, G., 23 September 2019, "Customer service 101", *Shopify Blog*, https://www.shopify.com/blog/customer-service

[50] Grossman, P., 20 September 2021, "Empowering your team: Kindness in customer service", *Zendesk*, https://relate.zendesk.com/articles/empowering-team-kindness-incustomer-service/

[51] 19 August 2020, *The Straits Times*, "More working from home feel stressed than those on Covid-19 front line: Survey", https://www.straitstimes.com/singapore/health/more-work-from-homers-feel-stressed-than-front-line-workers-singapore-survey-on

Sources

The essays in this book were originally published in *Today's Manager*: Kindness Is Good for Business (Issue 3, 2016); Think Positively, Act Kindly (Issue 4, 2016); Happiness at Work Is Not a Lost Cause (Issue 3, 2017); Are You Kind to Yourself? (Issue 2, 2018); Lead With Kindness: You Will Get Better Results (Issue 3, 2018); Why "Be Greater" Is Important for Our Society (Issue 4, 2019); What Do Kindness and Camaraderie Have in Common? (Issue 1, 2017); Building a Culture of Appreciation and Gratitude in the Workplace: Part 1 (Issue 4, 2017); Building a Culture of Appreciation and Gratitude in the Workplace: Part 2 (Issue 1, 2018); Integrating Locals and Foreigners in a Multicultural Workplace (Issue 4, 2021); Your Daily Job Can Make a Difference to Others (Issue 2, 2017); Support Local Artists Within Our Community (Issue 3, 2020); Appreciate Delivery Riders More to Support the Gig Economy (Issue 3, 2021); Don't Let Black Sheep Prevent Good Deeds (Issue 1, 2020); Humanising the Modern Workplace (Issue 1, 2019); Where Is Kindness in the Digital Age? (Issue 2, 2019); Can Excellent Customer Service Exist Without Kindness? (Issue 3, 2019); Practising Kindness@Work in the New Normal (Issue 1, 2021); Trust and Communication Help Remote Teams Thrive (Issue 2, 2020); Mental Health in the New Workplace Normal (Issue 2, 2021)

Image credits: Page 17 Shutterstock/Cagkan Sayin; p. 21 Shutterstock/ntkris; p. 25 Shutterstock/imtmphoto; p. 30 Shutterstock/Tom Wang; p. 35 Shutterstock/KieferPix; pp. 39 Singapore Kindness Movement; p. 44 Shutterstock/Momentum Fotograh; p. 48 Shutterstock/Rawpixel.com; p. 53 Shutterstock/Pormezz; p. 57 Shutterstock/Andrey_Popov; p. 63 Shutterstock/wk1003mike; p. 67 Shutterstock/Tang Yan Song; p. 72 Shutterstock/Dr David Sing; p. 77 Shutterstock/Rawpixel.com; p. 82 Shutterstock/TZIDO SUN; pp. 87 and 93 Shutterstock/fizkes; p. 98 Shutterstock/Vitalii Vodolazskyi; p. 109 Shutterstock/metamorworks

About the Author

Dr William Wan is the General Secretary of the Singapore Kindness Movement and a Justice of the Peace.

He is the Chairman of the Prison Fellowship Singapore, Vice President of the Singapore Scout Association and the Deputy Chairman of Farrer Park Hospital's Ethics Committee. Active in Project We Care, Hawkers' Committee, National Integration Working Committee, SG Cares Culture-building Committee and other non-profit projects, Dr Wan contributes in multiple ways to the greater good.

A public speaker and published author, his works include *Clearly Different* and *My Best with Honour*, written in support of the dyslexia and scouting community, respectively. His latest book is *Through the Valley: The Art of Living and Leaving Well*. He also contributes regularly to *The Straits Times*, *CNA Commentary* and Singapore Institute of Management's e-publication, *Today's Manager*.

Dr Wan has received several awards, including The Police Commissioners' Award and the Solicitor-General's Award in Canada, the Active Ageing Award from the Council of Third Age, the President's Volunteerism and Philanthropy Award, and the SSA Distinguished Service Award (Bronze).

ALSO BY SINGAPORE KINDNESS MOVEMENT

Marshall Cavendish Editions
ISBN 978-981-4974-23-3

Inspiring and heart-warming, this collection of 39 stories reminds us that there is kindness in everyone, and finds a silver lining in the Covid-19 pandemic. Instead of stepping away, these kind people stepped up – to show charity, compassion, and consideration for others.